the GAFFER

the GAFFER

Celeste Gainey

To Nancy —
Thank you for listening
to my poems. I hope
you enjoy reading
the rest!

Celeste Gainey

13 May 2015

Arktoi books | Pasadena, CA

Pittsburgh

Book design and layout by Jakki McCann

Library of Congress Cataloging-in-Publication Data
Gainey, Celeste.
  [Poems. Selections]
  The Gaffer / Celeste Gainey.
     p. cm
   ISBN 978-0-9890361-2-2 (pbk.)
   I. Title.
   PS3607.A35973A6 2015
   811'.6—dc23

                    2014036230

The Los Angeles County Arts Commission, the National Endowment for the Arts,
the Pasadena Arts & Culture Commission and the City of Pasadena Cultural Affairs
Division, the Los Angeles Department of Cultural Affairs, the Dwight Stuart Youth
Fund, Sony Pictures Entertainment and Ahmanson Foundation partially support
Red Hen Press.

First Edition
Published by Arktoi Books
An imprint of Red Hen Press, Pasadena, CA
www.arktoi.com
www.redhen.org

acknowledgments

Grateful acknowledgment is given to the editors and supporters of the print and online publications in which the following poems first appeared, sometimes in earlier versions:

BLOOM, "best boy," "in the days of early polyester," "more / less," "a field guide to muff diving"; *Columbia Poetry Review*, "black apricots"; *HEArt*, "in our nation's capital"; *Madroad: The Breadline Press West Coast Anthology*, "i always wanted a bird:"; *Pittsburgh City Paper*, "in my old west"; *Projector*, "before talkies," "nightmare [pre c.g.i.]," "skypan," "women in prison"; *Seven Kitchens Press Summer Kitchen Chapbook Series*, "in the early days of polyester," "between takes," "tail o' the cock," "once upon a time on all hallows' eve in gotham city," "albino nights," "flótti," "my dearest lover," "rush 501," "before lighting the gay men's s+m club," "god bless susan tyrrell," "in the lobby of the five star hotel," "vista del mundo," "fons et origo," "in the land of speculation & seismography"; *Voices from the Attic Volume XX*, "cameramen," "dog day afternoon"; *Wild Apples*, "fons et origo"; and *Writers at Work*, "flótti."

I would like to express huge and joyful gratitude to Arktoi Books and Eloise Klein Healy for believing in *the GAFFER* and giving it life. Big thanks to the terrific team at Red Hen Press: Kate Gale, Mark Cull, Alisa Trager, Jakki McCann, Sabrina Paparella, Luke Munson, William Chen, and my from-the-beginning taskmaster, Samantha Haney, for guiding this book into being. To Bec Young for the provocative cover design. My deep appreciation goes out to Dr. Ellie Wymard and the Carlow University MFA program, as well as the Madwomen in the Attic writing workshops, for the combination of goodwill and rigor that fostered the writing of so many of these poems.

I acknowledge and am indebted to the mighty writers who patiently read, listened to, and critiqued these poems in their gestation: mentor supernova Jan Beatty, as well as Judith Vollmer, Mary O'Donnell, Mark Roper, James Heaney, Niall Williams, Michael Coady, Nancy Krygowski, and Joy Katz. To Dorianne Laux, Charles Flowers, Aaron Smith, Ron Mohring, Adam Czernowski, Terry Wolverton, Leslie Mcilroy, Jane McKinley, and Heidi Johannesen Poon for their early encouragement. To Eve Eliot for pushing me toward the poetry cliff. To my insightful, close friends in both NY and LA: Nancy Leff, Leslie Robbins, Lynn Birks, Judith Wit, Amanda Pope, and Cabell Smith, who devoted many evenings to providing invaluable feedback and soul sustenance; to the many, many others on both coasts who have rallied me on, and, of course, my new poetry family in Pittsburgh—all yinz!—for welcoming me from afar with open arms. Your support means the world to me, but none more than Elise D'Haene, my alpha and omega, the one who is forever, who sees it all.

Finally, to my union brothers and sisters in Local 52, IATSE, you have given me a world to write about; I'm only sorry it has taken me so long to get around to it.

for Eloise Klein Healy

table of contents

the GAFFER

**once upon a time
on all hallows' eve
in gotham city**

A Weegee full moon
exposes the Dada
black cat and Quasimodo

they promenade
down
5th Avenue

wearing
their souls
on their sleeves

on the southeast corner of 31st
an Idaho potato
hails a taxi

1

... and the beauty of parking garages illuminated
in the night

—Eleni Sikelianos

pastoral w/ stars

The thing I'll never write is the green leaf
with its rubbery-hard veins.
                                    —Jan Beatty

Once when I was little, camping
for the first time, the strangeness of lying
on the damp, bumpy earth, the musky
tang of excitement zipping through
as I lay back and said *yes*!
to the heaping constellations above me—
stars popping & pummeling down
that *zipping*—the stars shooting through me
over & over—*e-l-e-c-t-r-i-c l-i-g-h-t o-r-c-h-e-s-t-r-a!*

Years later, fresh & hip & living in the City,
I got punched out by some bitch on a bike;
couldn't see her squeezing through beside the taxi,
opened my door right into her—*spokes.*
Et voila! as my buddy Michel would say—
she punched me! A clean one straight to the kisser.
Head snapped back. *Stars everywhere!*
Right there in naked daylight. Blinking all over,
a dizzy pop art stencil, a Sunday comic strip swirl
shooting through me.

i light lucy

I have the balls to know what she wants:
#34 flesh pink   inkies   4 of them
key/fill/hair/obie;
diffusion on the key
bounce the fill
flag the hair,
focus the obie   hard—
penetrate the eyes
                    to glisten & mesmerize.

Hair, a five-alarm,
lips of leaping flames,
blue eyes burning through
                    the bullshit—
& the voice, by now,
smoky   deep   demanding.

Always make up
in the best light,
                    Lucy tells me,
then demand
the same for your close-up.

my gay dad

buys corsages & boutonnieres on holidays,
first-class tickets to exotic locations,
imported lingerie, designer dresses,
for his wife; drum sets & electric trains,
even a pony for the kids.

He wears bespoke suits,
drives a Jaguar Mark VII,
can't stop renovating the house.
When mom's favorite hand lotion goes out of business,
he buys the company and makes it himself.

As Santa, we leave him a fifth of Chivas and a pack
of Benson & Hedges on the custom coffee table;
unwrapped toys, books, and records
artfully arranged—he transforms
the living room into a department store.

The year I am six,
Santa brings me the Broadway soundtrack
to Cole Porter's "Anything Goes."
I play it over & over, singing along—

now heaven knows—

best boy

The chief assistant to the gaffer on a movie or television set.
There are no "best girls" per se.

—IMDB Glossary

At the age of three
I tell my mother:
When I grow up, I'm going to be a man.
Like Pancho in *The Cisco Kid*:
high-heeled boots, a six-shooter.
Halloween, I'm a pirate with a hook,
in the Christmas pageant I insist on the Nutcracker
or Mouse King, never Marie.

Eighth grade, girls talk:
Who will get married? Make a good mother?
Not one can see me as a wife with kids.
It hurts a little to hear I'm not like them.
I'm a boy in a kilt and knee socks—
When I grow up, I'm going to play the field.

In high school I meet a boy
I either love or want to be.
He wears madras shorts, crosses his legs elegantly,

holds his Winston like a lady.
One day in a crowded elevator as a joke
he yells *Fuck, fuck, fuck!*
All you ever want to do is fuck! Who do you think I am—Superman?
No, I say, *I'm Superman!*
You're Lois Lane.

Just out of film school,
I apply for membership in the Union.
All the Local 52 boss wants to know—
can I carry *horsecock* same as any man?
All I want to know—will he let me join his band of brothers,
be Best Boy—apprentice
to Vinnie Delaney, Milty Moshlak, Dusty Wallace, Dickie Quinlan:
set their spider-boxes, haul their 4-aught,
flag their barn doors, trim their brute arcs,
run their stingers, scrim their broads,
wrap their 9-light fays;
let them make me a man.

the first autograph

the gaffer gets
(as a giggling kid)
is in Kerr's Sporting Goods
on Wilshire Blvd.
It's Jackie Cooper.
                He's looking at rifles.

before talkies

Back when men wear handkerchiefs
in their breast pockets,
I press a crisp bright square
over my hidden heart
for you.

It looks snappy
against the imported alpaca
of my sport jacket,
the collar of my very white polo shirt
spread open, à la Billy Haines,
the tan of my smooth skin peeking through.

An actor of the silent era,
I learn to be manly & discreet,
never disclosing our desire
for each other's sameness,
how you give it to me—exactly
the way I want.

But then there's that afternoon
at the lawn party, in front of L.B.'s guests
when the shuttlecock glances your eye

and I leap to you,
a lioness to her cub,

pluck my handkerchief
to dress your wound
and like that,
    just like that—
        the world stops.

in my old west

There are quail.
Each day, a line or two of them marching under
their topknots beneath the eucalyptus. And vultures—
buzzards we call them, sweeping overhead.
Some poor animal's dead in the field, my mother says,
then calls me in from the yard where I am crouched
on the blacktop—watching
the quick beat of a lizard's heart.
My brother strings my life-size Davy Crockett doll
up on a eucalyptus branch, breaks its neck.
The hard plastic face smashed in.
Under the peeling trees
I dig a pool in the sand, get the hose,
fill it with water. Run inside. Pull on my bathing suit.
Rush back. The pool is gone.
My father has the eucalyptus felled.
They're too messy. Roots too shallow.
They might collapse on the house.
He rolls a green lawn over the sand.
The field next door becomes a big house with a big gate.
The lines of quail march into fog. Crows come.
First to the olive tree, then to the walnut—sleek black
flapping, cawing into the day.

rush 501

I remember buying my first pair
on St. Mark's Place in '71

in some vintage clothing store
you had to walk up stairs to enter,

Joe Cocker—or maybe Leon Russell
blasting on the outdoor speakers.

The Holy Grail: 501s, brass button fly,
washed-out watercolor blue,

worn corners on the right hip pocket
where a wallet had been carried,

a slight cumulus cleft to the left
of the crotch, where he had stashed his bulge.

Putting them on was weird, a crazy rush;
like trying on the groove of a missing person,

something right and wrong at the same time—
an instant sex change operation.

I wore my 501s home on the 747,
with rough-out cowboy boots, poor-boy T-shirt,

midnight blue velvet blazer with wide lapels.
My mother took one look, knew something was up;

saw the groove of a missing person,
something wrong but right at the same time.

vista del mundo

I considered that the homes that people
live in exactly describe their lives.
—Douglas Sirk

I grow up on the front of a postcard,
the Riviera of the U.S. they call it,
the town of the newly wed & nearly dead,

the cemetery by the sea.
Every morning the serene Pacific
is the first thing I see as it lies a mile

or so down from my hilltop window;
the Channel Islands massing
in the distance like those photos

of gleaming warships in the Bay of Pigs.
Our surefire defense, we like to say,
against tsunami, or rogue tidal wave.

On the other side, the blue and pink
Santa Ynez Mountains rise up to hold
back as much of outside reality

as is geologically possible.
This is where my brother fixates on
Hitler and rock 'n' roll, while my father,

who bought this hilltop of post-WWII nirvana,
grows a brain tumor the size of an alien's fist
and drinks himself to death.

My brother obsessively archives 45s
in his grey-on-grey bedroom, visualizes
the death of our mother.

My sister and I, suspended
in pastel isolation, stare
at the blood-orange sunset.

i always wanted a bird:

a sombrero, cowboy boots, and button-up jeans like a boy;
a coloring book history of the United States, a burro (not a donkey),
a mother-of-pearl accordion; the ceremonial Indian headdress, the bamboo
spear with the big rubber tip, the ochre dress with stripes going the wrong way;
my father to stop drinking, my sister to protect me, my brother to disappear;
a hickory deluxe burger & chocolate chip shake at Petersen's Drive-In, spare ribs
& potato salad from Puppo's Delicatessen on my birthday.

I always wanted a canary:
the best grades in the class, white buck saddle shoes, Kennedy for President;
to be a tennis champion, save my mother from my brother, be the Governor
of California, head of Time Inc.; to not be fat, to be better at math, escape
to boarding school, ride my bike casually, tan easily & live on the beach at Malibu;
in a penthouse at the Beverly Hilton, in the Monsanto House of Tomorrow at Disneyland,
at The Plaza like Eloise; to drink Tiki punch at Trader Vic's, eat sweet butter
on date-nut bread at Bullock's Wilshire, Cobb salad at The Brown Derby.

I always wanted a canary in a round silver cage:
to fly first class, wear a tie & waistcoat, make money
but not care, be famous, but not too, be the woman (and man) of my dreams;
be born at the end of the nineteenth century, live in the demimonde of Paris,
The New York School in the fifties, La Nouvelle Vague in the sixties;
to love someone as much as my mother, be like the lilies of the field,

a pilgrim at The Ganges; to walk the sleepless streets of Greenwich Village,
the groomed pathways of the Champs de Mars, the icy avenues of Reykjavik;
live in isolation, die sooner rather than later, erase myself.
I always wanted a canary in a round silver cage, singing.

2

we take the silver way along the rocks
—Frank O'Hara

the gaffer

lamplighter
chief lighting technician
the DP's go-to guy

dispenser of gaffer's tape
brute arc myths
day for night & the anti-auteur theory

transposer of sun/shadow
nuancer of mood
romancer of stars:

wears a train engineer's jumpsuit
Rod Laver tennies
cutoffs & T-shirt that says "Strip 'n' Screw"

drives a panel van with blacked-
out windows, a hunky T-Bird
back to Levittown

calls you on Christmas weeping
wants to get into your pants
be forgiven right away

doesn't want the job to end
go home
be a regular joe—

lets no one see
she's under pressure
makes them believe

she can light the scene in the john
single bare bulb hanging down
let the eyes go black

in the days of early polyester

you don't know yet you are flammable;
jars of Miracle Whip, tubs of Polly-O in the fridge.
Your moral imperative on ice, the vertical blinds rattling shut,
sleek sofa of solid kerosene resisting your body's impression.
You keep saying, *Cotton, cotton, the touch, the feel of cotton*,
but you are drawn to the slinky boy shirt with the Kandinsky-like
print, fancy your stubbled sideburns whiskering
the top of its Byronesque collar—long points gesturing toward
no-tits torso, slim hips, bell-bottomed legs, Frye boots.
It feels like Velveeta against your skin, something you might
scrape off with the blade of your Swiss Army knife.
It seems to reject you. Still, you can't stop
parading your shirt through Washington Square Park
in the hot afternoon sun—looking for combustion.

more / less

more gay
than queer
more queer
than lesbian
less lesbian
than girl
more girl
than woman
less woman
than man
more boy
than bi
less bi
than butch
more butch
than dyke
more dyke
than trans
less trans
than faggot
more fag
than bulldagger
more bulldagger
than top

less top
than bottom
least top
no top
more bottom
less 's'
more 'm'
more bottom
more bottom
less homo
more sexual

cameramen

some will leave you alone
some will tell you where to plug it in
some will respect you
some will only talk sports
some will call you *baby legs*

some will not know how to talk to you
not even *hello*

dog day afternoon

(1975, Sidney Lumet, dir.)

Medium shot:
NYPD blue & white pulls up,

Leon, Sonny's trans lover, emerges
from the back—gaunt, matted fro,

flimsy hospital robe, tired mascara
racooning his eyes.

Take after take
the door flings open, its window flares,

no matter which way/how many times
I tweak the flag on the fill.

I feel a hand on my shoulder.
I turn to find Mr. Lumet

at full attention.
What's the problem?

I start to explain.
He raises his hand,

I'll cut before that, he says,
Don't worry about it.

Then looking into me,
It doesn't matter.

the '70s:

size 6 brown & black houndstooth pants
pegged 2" cuff/brown alligator belt
British brogans/fringed tongue flap/crepe soles
green & putty argyle socks
camel's hair shawl collar cardigan
braided brown leather buttons
cream-colored silk shirt/stiff collar & cuffs
vintage Thanksgiving tie from *Early Halloween*
w/ little doodles—turkey, peace pipe, Indian
headdress—tumbling down
I teach myself to make the knot
in front of the bathroom mirror in my first apartment
on west 9th between 5th and 6th
ease it up snug into the collar/tight to my throat
so it looks authentic—like I do this every day
carefully pull on my replica USN bomber jacket
the age of innocence is upon me
mouton fur collar up
tan leather driving gloves
aviator Ray-Bans
walking up 5th Avenue
I am one with my people
history is ours for the making

from green river cemetery

after Frank O'Hara

The late
summer light still bright enough
to read the epitaph on your
headstone and I am feeling curious.
I slip a lone question
into the bluebird's beak
and he is off!

*How did you know this graveyard
is where the party would carry on?*

To the others gathered in your
company:
to Pollock to Krasner,
de Kooning to Kline, Ernst
to Geldzahler, to Patsy Southgate et al:
grace to be born and live as variously as possible!

Over your silver shoulder
the improving stars continue
to devour your poems

flash them onward.

      And here you are again   the center
of all these beautiful people—you
and the bluebird's question—
Still! Imagine!

the gaffer at papaya king

Yankee Doodle Dandy (1942, Michael Curtiz, dir.)

It's 1:34 on Wednesday
& I'm standing in line at
Papaya King 86th & 3rd
the blinking digital watch
on the guy in front of me
a reminder that here I am
in my blue shirt & blue jeans
on this brightest of blue days
in June wanting nothing
more than a burger & large
papaya juice the hot circuit
of life pulsing through me out
onto the honking street & back
again when the guy with the watch
looks up from his paper
no international news
he says *what's the matter*
with this country don't they know
there's life beyond Hollywood?
I want to tell him
the DVD's still on & playing
the one with Jimmy Cagney

tap dancing in his red white
& blue but it's sure to be
over any minute
in the meantime could he hurry
up & order   *please*
in case that moment is now.

nightmare [pre-c.g.i.]

The Wiz (1978, Sidney Lumet, dir.)
HAIR (1979, Milos Forman, dir.)

The World Trade Center
is Emerald City, electric's
loading in, miles of mis-
labeled cables; I keep
shouting into my walkie-talkie,
We need to get organized!
A block-long generator
catches fire, FDNY shows up—
tries to shut us down—
You making a movie here?
So many 9-light fays needed,
we fly more in from London,
the fountain's somehow
a dance floor but the lights
below—going Green! Red!
Gold!—don't dim, the
Lightflex won't work.
The night's cold & long,
wind whipping the towers,
Michael & Diana huddle
in Eddie Bauer down,

Nipsy Russell's in agony—
his Tin Man costume's too
tight, Toto's never in the shot.
Mr. Lumet doesn't care,
he's in the middle of
a divorce, he's not waiting
for some mutt; the yellow
brick road's made of
crappy linoleum, we're
tired & confused.
I want to lie down
in the warmth of
the 9-lights blasting
the lobby of Tower 1;
HAIR's shooting
up in Central Park—
our crew's sure it's
going to be a flop.

before lighting the gay men's s+m club:

Homosexuals (1979, *ABC News Close-Up*, Helen Whitney, dir.)

It's the morning after the night before.
The twisted Twinkie Defense,
the White Night Riots—and now—here,
7am, Sunday morning in the Castro.
Back of my van wheeled up to the rear entrance,
my cable and lights in big hampers waiting
to be off-loaded.

Leaning against the van with my producer,
strapping on my tool belt, I'm thinking about the breaker
panel, whether or not I'll have to tie in.
So tired after it all.
There's one more location, one more day
of shooting. I have today to pre-light; the rest
of the crew is off, no doubt sleeping away
most of it, lucky bastards. Still,
I'm on Golden Time.

She's telling me it's going to be
the lyrical sequence of this ABC documentary
on gay life in America—just the empty club.
No talking heads or hunky bodies
in bondage, but *something experimental, haunting.*

She urges me to *be creative,* make
lots of shadows—poetry!

The manager comes out.
We have to sign releases holding them harmless
for, among other things, "any injury to bodies
or equipment resulting from slipping and/or sliding on the floor."
I look down at my beat-up Rod Laver's, examine the soles,
almost smooth; the palms of my work gloves too, shiny
and slick with wear; think about my funky rental ladder,
the traction of its four worn black rubber feet.
I sign on the dotted line,
cross over the metal threshold into night.

in our nation's capital

On the occasion of viewing the AIDS Memorial Quilt
October 1992, Washington, D.C.

You motion for me to come sit on your lap.
You carry me to the bedroom.

Undress me. Lay me down
on crisp hotel sheets—

a soft quilt for mothering
in a place where there is no mothering

—only monuments to neglect & regret
where we tread the grassy mall

the length & breadth of
Silence = Death.

No soft breast to suck
as I do yours now:

you are above me pressing
/grinding down on my cunt.

You pull your tit away
turn me over/

lift my buttocks
spread my cheeks.

Then your warm spit
/your tongue rimming me.

I'm on my knees now
rocking hard to your rhythm.

This is church;
the motherfucking/big-ass

National Cathedral in the dead of night;
Black Mass candles blazing,

dead saints watching, mute
& unblinking, from their pedestals,

hollowed eyes of marble politicians
peeping through the stained glass.

You the butch high priestess of too much sorrow
/me the submissive penitent

longing to feel your pain—take it.
Pull it deep inside.

We're not supposed to be here
/doggie-style in our nation's capital,

the quilt tending away now,
undulating bodies in retreat—

your aching fist
an anchor at the bottom of me.

3

oh. thirst. oh. pride.

i am dying in lala in a sunblaze in
a dream dreamt then forsaken

—Wanda Coleman

albino nights

Grand Canyon (1991, Lawrence Kasdan, dir.)

In the City of Angels, the sun never sets—
instead there's Sunset Boulevard.

Strip of liquored up incandescence
permanently switched-on,

its half-haze hovering the basin,
preempting the stars over Cielo Drive.

It's impossible
to sleep here. Not impossible to dream.

So you do.
Next thing you know you're exiting the 10

at La Cienega, heading for the hills.
Some guy in a wife-beater and flip-flops,

plastic bag of oranges in one hand,
maps to the dead and dying in the other,

stands on the corner, the same frame
in the same B movie you walked out on years ago.

You drive and drive the florid landscape. Finally
pull up to a shady bungalow on the Hollywood Flats.

The door opens. The lights don't switch on.
No matter, the street lamp's metal halide oozes in.

You find a tiny bedroom at the back of the house,
bed snugged up to an open window, lie down,

inhale the ether of the sweet night jasmine.
You feel like Dee, the Mary-Louise Parker character

in *Grand Canyon*, masturbating
amid the white funnels and whirring sounds of copters.

The butch neighbor girl pulls up in her 4x4,
slams a screen door inches from your head.

"You're dead to me," her disembodied voice announces—
"Dead to me."

early sunday morning

you fuck me first thing,
we talk about our dreams,

throw clothes on, walk the empty
partied-out sidewalk of Santa Monica Blvd

to the 24 hr newsstand on Westbourne
for *The Times*, backtrack

down and over a block,
upstairs in the strip mall, next

to the Ramada Inn, where
those sweet scrawny queer boys

seem to be playing restaurant—
treating us like their best customers.

We are the only ones here,
among so many yellow placemats,

when you tell me you love me
for the first time.

You order eggs over easy,
well-done hash browns, crispy bacon,

side of buttered whole wheat toast.
I do the same, afraid to lose you.

skypan

A primitive contraption, one of hundreds
hanging from scaffolding high above

the football-length sound stage,
crafted to clone the ambient light of sky

but really, only a round, shallow pan
painted white on the inside, Mole

Richardson red on the outside.
Its 2k or 5k lamp screwed into a socket

attached to the rim, hot rays bouncing
off its milky circumference and falling,

filling a long silken sock extending down,
diffusing onto every surface, into every shadow.

In this pretend universe we work hard
to create the perfect weather:

a knockout summer day right now
but soon a darkening—

then rain;
cue the wind machines—Harvey Keitel.

what the oscar-winning actress says:

When I observe people being coupled,
I see too many compromises.

But
invariably there will be
some on-set gaffer

who will have caught my eye.

To my very best friends
I refer to her as my boyfriend.
I never touch her. Never talk
to her even. She has no idea
she's my boyfriend.

This is much easier than actually
having to deal with somebody.

under western skies

Each morning I wake into the Gold Rush.
Pull on my checked flannel shirt, my chinos w/ suspenders,
copper-toed boots minus the laces, my lucky bandana
around my neck.

I take the pickaxe down from the wall. Head for the hills.

Oh, I know. I know exactly where to go today—where there's gold.
I stop to drink from my sweating canteen. Look up. Squint.

Someone's already working my claim—calmly,
methodically. She smiles, waves *her* lucky bandana,
pretends to mop the glow from her brow.
The heat of all that gold beating down
& I'm caught standing in the pitch of the peak, unearthed
in the shadow of its reflection:

     cloud, the light it shrouds;

        the fortune herein.

tail o' the cock

Where the margarita made its debut.
There was one on La Cienega,
another on Ventura Blvd in the Valley.
Neon feathers animating up, then down,
the booze always on the rocks, the steak,
three-inch filet—bloody,
onion rings on top, an Idaho,
baked in gold tinfoil swelling sour cream
& chives, on the side.

You might stop before the long drive home.
Pretty boy valets in cropped red jackets
tempt you out in the porte-cochere.
Inside—a moment—dusk sifts in,
the maître d' at his podium, little pillow of light
on his face, oversize menus, flocked covers,
tassels swinging, he ushers you into the low-
ceilinged labyrinth; lodge of plush booths tucked
into nocturnal alcoves,

glow of tiny table lanterns bearding
the famous faces. Everyone here
to be seen, but hiding;
the men look like Vic Damone:

manicured nails, silk suits & alligator loafers;
the women like Angie Dickinson:
too blonde, too beautiful, too smart for him.
Two tables over, a crown of fire—
the cherries jubilee has been served.

god bless susan tyrrell

Fat City (1972, John Huston, dir.)

Oma, the unzipped sherry-loving lush at the end of the bar in Huston's *Fat City*,
slurring, *do you know who your friends are?* Half-falling into the arms of Keach's
you can count on me Billy Tully, has-been boxer; Conrad Hall's moth-pocked light
slanting in high and honeyed, dust showers and beatific shine cloaking the two dreamers
in this Loserville of late afternoon San Joaquin Valley, 1972. Days talking gibberish on a bar
stool, nights ranting in a rented room. Forgiveness, if not redemption, somewhere lost
down the road.
At the Oscars that year, Sacheen Littlefeather, former *Miss American Vampire*, refuses
Best Actor for the protesting Godfather, Marlon Brando, then becomes a *Playboy*
centerfold; Keach doesn't even get a nod. Tyrrell gets nominated as *Best Supporting*
but doesn't win; Eileen Heckert does, for *Butterflies Are Free*—forgotten now.
You're the only son of a bitch worth shit in this place, Oma tells Tully, *these others,*
I wouldn't ask 'em the time of day.

my dearest lover,

Greetings from Bikini Atoll. Boy, is it hot here!
And, oddly, not a speck of sun. Wish I were with you

in the snowy northeast. You'd never believe
the sights—these clouds! Wow! Big as giant

mushrooms! The sand, scorched & smoky,
too hot to walk on, unless you're an aspiring yogi,

which, as you know, I am not!
The skin-flayed natives are kind & quiet—

too quiet, even for me. They rarely speak,
but draw strange pictographs in the angry

sand with long sticks that catch fire & combust
to ash before they can finish whatever

it is they have to say. The silence is like none
I've ever heard. Just the faintest crackle-

crackle of burning sand & flesh, and always
a low whoosh-whoosh, the kind of sound I recall

the x-ray machine making at the Mayo Clinic,
its long shadow passing over, exposing the dead in me.

Ridiculous, isn't it, how full of sound silence can be,
even out here, lost in the Pacific,

a speck at the flaming end of things—
I wish I could hear your voice.

dream of cali

A shaggy Baldessari is showing me his lousy shots
of National City, CA;

he tells me *THE SPECTATOR IS COMPELLED TO LOOK*
DIRECTLY DOWN THE ROAD

AND INTO THE MIDDLE OF THE PICTURE.
I'm smack *in* the picture:

first the blue—blank & flat rolling out
over the yuccas & sparkle plenty rooftops;

the blacktop melting down the hill away
from my trashed Van slip-ons

to the Cuyamacas—to *Gonesville.*
I feel no border between the landscape out there,

the landscape in here: arteries of decomposed granite
rooting me forever to this conceptual landfill,

making room for my little failures—
even in broad daylight.

All the flagstone-faced houses,
red-jacketed valets re-parking Ferraris.

First in one driveway. Then another.

l.a.**me n t**

my feet are cold

you are far
away   asleep already
in some other game show

                    snow on your tv

the streets are silent   empty

here   despite
the Bob Barker sun   the
people in costume

                    all the giveaway cars

maybe tomorrow

I can get away   once
& for all   make it slyly home
to you   *a winner!*

                    never look back

women in prison

(1974, *ABC News Close-Up*, Joseph DeCola, dir.)

at Alderson:

My Mickey Mouse watch says 3am.
The hum of charging batteries,
heaps of knotted cable
on a bad burgundy shag,
hands shredded from dicking
with the prison's tamper-proof fixtures.

Whatever's going down here,
it can't be seen. Thanksgiving
in the cafeteria, a Muzak melody—
Don't Fence Me In.

at Marysville:

Inmates are lined up with radios
TVs and toaster ovens—they think
I'm *that* kind of electrician. They
corner me in the hallway, want
my earrings, my tool belt, my job.

They know I'm the one who can
make them look like stars, so
they smile a lot, throw me kisses.

at Sybil Brand:

Joan Churchill, our camerawoman,
hand-holding her Eclair, shoots the strip
search in her moccasins, soundless
along shellacked linoleum—

New Year's Eve, I'm back in LA,
in a Safeway in Silver Lake.
Too brightly fluorescent,
everywhere I look
I see beautiful faces in lockup.

in the land of speculation & seismography

there are dwellings made of future:
low-slung eaves & camphor wood structures

unspooling the coast like chambered fog, clinging
to jutting scarps, glass-front cantilevers containing

lost Midwest revelers, unsuspecting
under ceilings of roiling ocean waves—

the first to make the scene, strike a pose
for modernity—sitting on air like stiffs, smiling at what—

the sea; they would learn quickly to eat
the whole enchilada with hot sauce,

sip margaritas in the afternoon,
listen nervously for *The Daylight* down

the tracks at the end of the day.
Hi-balls & hi-fi, haiku

of the no-ties, yes-*my* lifestyle,
if this was the price to be paid for never

waking to snow or leafless trees, walking
up stairs, growing grey hair—all eyes

ahead—boulevards of palm, dreams
of dichondra, horizons of flagstone; never mind

the hobos by the bird refuge, rattlers in the foothills,
children in the driveway, tremors on the fault line—

4

something elemental I cannot
get away from: it pursues me
across endless prosceniums, this
ball and chain of light.
—Anonymous

fons et origo

for Eugene Fracchia
1939–1988

People say things like:
Oh, you designed the lighting for Union Square Cafe?
That's where I got engaged!
You lit Gramercy Tavern? I love to go there. The lighting makes me look so good!
Sweet. But not what I want to hear.

In interviews if someone asks:
What would you like to light that you haven't yet?
I say—*a freeway.*
You'll stay awake on *my* stretch of interstate—
There'll be color, gesture, inclination—*flux*
You'll wonder *how did this happen?* Turn around.
Want to do *that* again.

Or the marsh grass at Louse Point:
to illumine those cattails kinetic—(in secret)—*without permission*—
washing indigo to vermillion to scarlet—*psychedelic light trip*—for one night only
(then run) like a tagger.

My friend Eugene was the one who asked:
Want to light my restaurant?
I did. Everyone came—the place caught fire. A star was born.

There I go again—dreaming *gesture, inclination*—
waking to *fire, star* instead.

My encounters with illumination:
exquisitely framed tableaux recalled
in a museum, like Vermeer still lifes on a wall;
still, all I really want is the ultra-white Dutch door, upper-half ajar,
slice of Turrell blue bleeding through.

woodland 7-2257

My mother is dead now as long as she was married—fifteen years.
Some days I just want to talk to her,

to reach for the cell phone she never knew, speed dial home:
1-805-682-2991 or, even farther back, WOodland 7-2257.

What would I say?
I no longer recall the sound of your voice—

although the apparition of it still comforts me
along with the signature on the flyleaf

of the 1948 edition of *Cooking By The Clock*
I go to whenever I need

to prove that I didn't dream you up.
There *was* a green phone with rotary dial

and curly cord on the inlaid antique desk in the den
and a white phone wall-mounted next to

the psychedelic Hendrix poster in the kitchen
and a beige phone on the faux Rococo nightstand in your bedroom

and a baby blue one somewhere—

> or was that a radio?

o   o   o

If I could have only one sure memory:

the Peace roses are in bloom.
Beyond, the Pacific blankets out,

sun staccatos through the white shutters
of the breakfast room.

You are seated at the round Saarinen table
in that bright '60s print dress

working a double-crostic.
The house fills with my ringing.

You rise to answer.

flótti

You can't pick papayas in Iceland
but you can stand in a forest of icicles,
listen to them crack,
skin hot as a Gauguin native;
fury of a vernal sun
beating.

There's a hotel where you lie
between sheets of ice, dreaming;
your igneous history oozing,
the earth yawning open
snap/crackle/pop
below.

Here in the white fire of absence
none will find you;
in the center of a lava field
you soak in the swelter,
on your lips, tiny flames of snow
burning.

a field guide to muff diving:

How we like it hard.
How the others like it I sometimes imagine.

But one thing to stop imagining, *please*—
is two chicks eating each other out.

That soggy old saw of lesbian sex
(mullets and the Indigo Girls)

is so Reagan-era eighties.
We may talk nice, look lipstick-sweet,

but the dykes I know
ball fists/strap on cocks

turn on backs/bellies
crack open cunts/lips/assholes—

bury the big hard-on—
blow it all to smithereens.

Why so much violence?
Why does pleasure carry pain inside?

Let's name it:
fury—

that's what two women breed in bed.
that's what we want/what we do/

feels like love.

the seventh avenue line

28th Street subway platform, stepping out from the #1 train.
T12 HO lamps, explosion-proof sleeves,

brash slashes brooding overhead—
icing the tiled walls,

the foyer/the lobby/the arcade/
what architects call *transition space*:

the terminal I'm always passing through
on my way to someplace else;

where the lighting can be brutal
because nobody's going to loiter

long enough to care if it glares.
But I do: my inner Spectra

forever seeking f8—*too bright*
is the heaven I'm after,

what I've lucked into down here—
[*not even an express stop*]

—whiteness that bleaches my brain,
washes me clean: *I am the Blazer!*

my step buoyant & sure,
my body fluorescent—ascending,

fresh & complete,
to the street.

black apricots

Sunday Bloody Sunday (1971, John Schlesinger, dir.)
The Tree of Wooden Clogs (1979, Ermanno Olmi, dir.)

Stood up for dinner by his bisexual lover, Peter Finch
listens achingly to *Così fan tutte* in *Sunday Bloody Sunday*—

he shares the young man knowingly with Glenda Jackson.
It's complicated. Until it's not.

What it feels like to sit slumped in the dusk
of an uptown theater one long Sunday afternoon

watching the humble feast in *The Tree of Wooden Clogs*,
your short life washing over you in silver waves—

you know this isn't real, but you want to close your eyes
let the images take you—

                          awaken to the familiarity of strange fruit:

a young Doris Day snares the plum role in a Wong Kar-wai film
and is made cool love to by Tony Leung Chiu-wai;

afterward she tenderly feeds him tiny black apricots balanced
on mother-of-pearl chopsticks.

in the lobby of the five star hotel

the line of light tucked into the ceiling is puckered;
little claws of grey pinching the glow at regular intervals.

Indicating they didn't do it right,
didn't overlap the lamps six inches, so the line

appears even, harmonious, uninterrupted.
How we like our light to be.

But the owner who spent the money
to build the recess in the first place didn't want

to spend any more to do it right,
to install continuous cold cathode or a low voltage strip.

Probably thought, who's going to look up there anyway?

Didn't realize the eye is attracted to disturbance
/disharmony: glimpsing the shadows as they gather

/grabby fingers of absence—can't help
but look up—

the gaffer's invocation

                    after the breaker
panel cover's off, Amprobe set, single-
or 3-phase, 3- or 4-wire determined,
lugs cordoned off w/ cardboard
to tie-in safely, not blow myself
against the bricks—but it's never
a sure thing—the lugs are big,
the spring clamps on the tie-ins tight,
their saw-toothed jaws impossible
to open with my small hand while standing
on a wooden apple box, one arm
behind my back, the other supposedly
executing the tie-in, dry-mouthed,
knock-kneed, sweating—who knows
to trust the Amprobe, what the fuck
its almighty scale is telling me anyway,
so I say, "It's a good day to die,"
my go-to mantra—within the intimate
confines of my blue-chevroned
coveralls—then use both hands.

between takes

Taxi Driver (1976, Martin Scorsese, dir.)
Columbus Circle, summer 1975

De Niro idles in his Checker. Cybill flirts behind
her Jackie-Os. Scorsese sucks oxygen from a tiny
tank trailed by an assistant. Albert Brooks hogs
the PA: *When using the moving sidewalk,*
please stand to the right, if you wish to pass, please
do so on the left. Over & over. Grips lay dolly track
for a shot we all know will never make the final cut
but will take most of the day to shoot.
     Me in my 501s & Mighty Mouse T-shirt,
20 feet up, work gloves & pliers protruding,
the brute arc light I tend sputters & hisses
beside me. Like that famous *New Yorker* cover
showing the world as seen from 9ᵗʰ Avenue—
the land of make believe rises up
to swallow me whole.
          I try to lean as if belonging against
the unsteady rungs of my ladder—oblivious
to the real world down there too—
passing me by; most, jaded New Yorkers,

their eyes on the prize, but maybe some
looking up & wondering *what's that girl doing
up there in the sky—flying so close to the sun?*
Some kind of myth. With pliers.

glossary

1K, 2K, 5K: 1,000-watt, 2,000-watt, 5,000-watt light sources.

4-aught (0000): largest diameter electrical cable used on a film set. Euphemistically referred to as *horsecock*.

9-light fay: luminaire with nine PAR lamps that may be controlled individually or together.

#34 flesh pink: a colored gel used in front of a luminaire to warm the source. Often used to enhance skin tone.

Amprobe: used to measure electrical current.

Baby legs: slang for a short-legged tripod; sometimes called a *hi hat*.

Barn doors: a set of metal flaps attached to a luminaire that can be adjusted to block or re-direct light.

Broad: rectangular luminaire emitting a wide, even distribution of light.

Brute arc: a high intensity carbon arc lamp used on early to mid-twentieth-century film sets, usually to fill or heighten the effect of sunlight. The carbon rods require *trimming* to maintain even illumination.

c.g.i.: computer generated imagery.

Cold cathode: continuous linear light source; a larger diameter version of neon.

DP: Director of Photography (also Cinematographer) on a feature film set.

Eclair: a brand of 16mm film camera favored by documentary cinematographers in the '70s and '80s.

f8: a particular aperture opening on a camera lens.

Fill or fill light: a secondary light source used to fill the key light.

Flag: a device used to block light.

Horsecock: see entry for **4-aught**.

Inkie: a low-wattage, Fresnel-lensed luminaire designed to light small areas; often used to fill the eyes.

Key/fill/hair: the tried-and-true lighting technique for illuminating a close-up, involving a direct source called the *key light*, a secondary source, often diffused, called the *fill light*, and an accent light used to highlight the hair, called the *hair light*.

Lightflex: pre-flashing device for color film.

Low-voltage strip: a linear light source comprised of many small low-voltage lamps spaced at regular intervals to provide even illumination, usually concealed in soffits, under cabinets and shelves.

Metal halide: a high-intensity discharge (HID) light source, commonly used in roadway lighting.

Obie: a small light source, usually an *inkie*, used to fill the face and create sparkle in the eyes. Named for the actress Merle Oberon, on whose face and eyes the light source was first used.

Spectra: brand name of a commonly used light meter.

Spider box: electrical junction box with several outlets.

Stinger: slang for an electrical extension cord.

T12 HO lamp: a 1.5-inch diameter, high-output fluorescent lamp.

Tie-in(s): to access the main source of an electrical distribution system directly; also the equipment used to do so.

notes

"i light lucy" refers to an appearance by Lucille Ball at the Museum of Broadcasting in New York City in 1984.

"best boy" is for Richard Krulikowski. Vinnie Delaney, Milty Moshlak, Dusty Wallace, Dickie Quinlan were legendary gaffers in Local 52 of the IATSE, New York City.

"before talkies": Billy Haines was a silent screen star whose career was cut short because he refused to deny his homosexuality. He then went on to become a celebrated interior designer.

"the '70s": *Early Halloween* was a great vintage clothing shop on 9th Avenue in Chelsea owned by Joyce Ostrin—she treated her customers like family.

"from green river cemetery" uses some words from Frank O'Hara's poems, "A Pleasant Thought from Whitehead" and "Autobiographia Literaria."

"nightmare [pre-c.g.i.]": pre-c.g.i. refers to the fact that all special effects on *The Wiz* were executed manually or mechanically—before the evolution of computer generated imagery.

"before lighting the gay men's s+m club" is set against the backdrop of the "White Night Riots" that erupted in San Francisco in May of 1979 after Dan White's assassination of

Supervisor Harvey Milk and Mayor George Moscone was judged to be merely voluntary manslaughter.

"in our nation's capital," "early sunday morning," and "my dearest lover," are for Elise D'Haene.

"what the oscar-winning actress says:" makes use of dialogue from an interview with Melissa Leo in *The New York Times Magazine*, September 16, 2012.

"Oscar®" is a trademark of the Academy of American Motion Pictures Arts & Sciences. Its use in *the GAFFER* acknowledges all legal rights and restrictions attendant to the enforcement of this trademark.

"tail o' the cock" was an iconic Los Angeles restaurant from the 1940s through the 1980s.

"dream of cali" makes use of lines from John Baldessari's *National City* series.

"in the land of speculation & seismography" is for my parents, Walt & Pat, pioneers of the West.

"between takes": *Taxi Driver* was the second time a woman worked on an IATSE (union) feature film in a technical capacity; the first was *Dog Day Afternoon*.

biographical note

Celeste Gainey is the author of the chapbook *In the land of speculation & seismography* (Seven Kitchens Press, 2011), runner-up for the 2010 Robin Becker Prize. She holds an MFA in Creative Writing/Poetry from Carlow University and a BFA in Film & Television from the Tisch School of the Arts at New York University. The first woman admitted to the International Alliance of Theatrical Stage Employees (IATSE) as a gaffer, Gainey has spent over thirty-five years working with light—as a gaffer for motion pictures and as an architectural lighting designer.